Hunting the Boar

Beverley Bie Brahic is a poet and translator. Her translation of selected poems by Francis Ponge, *Unfinished Ode to Mud* (CBe, 2008), was shortlisted for the Popescu Prize for European poetry in translation; her translations of poems by Apollinaire under the title *The Little Auto* (CBe, 2012) won the Scott Moncrieff Prize. Her previous collection of poetry, *White Sheets* (CBe, 2012), was shortlisted for the Forward Prize.

also by Beverley Bie Brahic

POETRY
White Sheets
Against Gravity
Unfinished Ode To Mud by Francis Ponge (translation)
The Little Auto by Guillaume Apollinaire (translation)
The Present Hour by Yves Bonnefoy (translation)
The Anchor's Long Chain by Yves Bonnefoy (translation)

SELECTED PROSE TRANSLATIONS
Rue Traversière by Yves Bonnefoy
Twists and Turns in the Heart's Antarctic by Hélène Cixous
Hemlock by Hélène Cixous
Hyperdream by Hélène Cixous
Manhattan by Hélène Cixous
Dream I Tell You by Hélène Cixous
The Day I Wasn't There by Hélène Cixous
Reveries of The Wild Woman by Hélène Cixous
Portrait of Jacques Derrida as a Young Jewish Saint by Hélène Cixous
Geneses, Genealogies, Genres and Genius by Jacques Derrida
This Incredible Need to Believe by Julia Kristeva

OTHER
the eye goes after
(limited edition artist's book of digital images by Susan Cantrick
accompanying twenty poems by Beverley Bie Brahic)

Beverley Bie Brahic

HUNTING THE BOAR

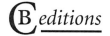

First published in 2016
by CB editions
146 Percy Road London W12 9QL
www.cbeditions.com

The right of Beverley Bie Brahic to be identified as author
of this work has been asserted in accordance
with the Copyright, Designs and Patents Act, 1988

Printed in England by Blissetts, London W3 8DH

ISBN 978–1–909585–18–8

for Michel and the kids, with love

ACKNOWLEDGEMENTS

Thank you to the editors of the following magazines, where versions of these poems first appeared: *Ambit*; *Field*; *The Hudson Review*; *Malahat Review*; *The Manchester Review*; *Notre Dame Review*; *Partisan*; *PN Review*; *Poetry Ireland*; *Poetry Review*; *Queen's Quarterly*; *Salamander*; *Times Literary Supplement.*

The description of fig tree varieties in 'Two Varieties of Common Figs' was plucked from the website www.galgoni.com/ENG/ Fotos_Maxi/016.htm.

Special thanks to generous friends and first readers for their suggestions and objections, and to the MacDowell Colony for the gift of time and companionship.

Contents

HUNTING THE BOAR

Arrivals

Let's unpack the rental car
we scratched backing into the old stable –
fit for a nag, that door.

Let's make the bed –
here's the wardrobe
lode of sheets that Tantine mended,

drenched in thyme and naphthalene,
darns palpable
as scabs on kids' skinned knees.

Let's drag those chairs out
to the garden, *hortus now conclusus*
figs fermenting in the dirt

(don't for god's sake track them in),

let's ponder dust
on emptied bottles,
maman-belle's unfinished canvas,

the antic anti-heroes –*Tintin*, *Lucky Luke* –
let's uncork
this green bottle of last year's *Cave Saint Marc*,

and wind the clock
that doesn't work
– but first, come on, I made the bed.

Found, in the Mailbox

'We'll be in Marseilles
when you arrive, but
you know where the key is.
The pears are ripe – eat
or the wasps will:

cup each pear in the palm
of your hand, and squeeze
gently. If it comes
it's ripe. If not, wait
a day and try again.

Don't let them go to waste.'

Continuities: Gifts

Claude pounding on the front door.
Scrabble-board click of the eternal tile
as two by two
you lope downstairs. Key chatter. Hinge grumble.

Claude bagged a blackbird
he's plucked and skewered for lunch
A few eggs from my yard,

a nugget of black truffle
to perk up your omelet . . .
Traffic continuo up to the castle

where German soldiers marched
villagers yesterday
years ago the road is dirt

Claude's dad bangs on the door
a bucket of almonds, the wife's Picholine olives . . .
maybe even
a portion of Meleager's boar.

A Recipe

In the XVIIth century two brothers from Italy, the Picholinis, settled in the Gard region of southern France. They devised a recipe for making green olives fit to eat:

'Pick the olives, still green, in September. Wash them, discarding stems and leaves. Soak them in a solution of ashes and water for 5 or 6 hours; then rinse them morning and night for a week: the water should stay clear for at least 4 hours. Prepare a brine of salt, thyme, rosemary, a bay leaf and some fennel, and strain into an earthenware jar. Add the olives. Wait at least 5 days before eating.'

Hunting the Boar

'He was proud to be a peasant,'
Claude keeps saying.
'He never aspired
to anything else.' With the butt
of his pocket knife
Claude tamps his pipe. This afternoon

they packed his cousin
off to Carpentras hospital,
ambulance's blue light darting
through vineyards and orchards.
'*Come and visit,*
his wife'd say – but I don't know,

him in that chair, the Parkinson's,
do you think he'd want to see me?'
It's New Year's Eve.
Claude's transistor squats
on worn red oilcloth,
a small Bakelite god

coughing up static
pensions, health insurance,
fresh graves in the Balkans.
It could be 1940,
the wireless reassembled
from its cache in the loft,

which still has a stall
for the draft horse, meat,

a row of hutches
for his mother's rabbits, a trap
to let out the ghosts
to graze on the threshing floor.

It could be the year the Germans
herded villagers
to the riverbank, and Louise Raymond,
'the Alsacienne', told them
they had old men; the maquisards
withdrawn to the cave-riddled hills

Petrarch climbed, returning
by moonlight to Malaucène,
'The day was long,
the air was mild, the Alps far off
covered in snow.'
Instead they torched the castle.

It's 1999, President Chirac
on the radio. Wind whines
in a stovepipe elbow,
worries a warp in the shutters.
Claude toasts almonds
from the rickety tree out back

whose white bloom
is winter's wager of spring.
We crack and eat
and listen to the mistral
trying to come in.
Shells mound in front of us.

'Tell us about the boar –'
So Claude lights up, blows
a scrim of smoke: 'We were posted
below the dam,
in Roger's vines. Suddenly
the boar appears – she –

c'est une femelle – stops
and sniffs suspiciously' –
as Claude takes aim
and fires, once. He shows us
the caliber shell. 'A young one
who'd never had babies – !'

His eyes crinkle
like the sparks that leap
from the firebox when you toss in
your handful of shells –
'You'd never believe
how tender her flesh was.'

Shyly he lifts his cap,
rakes his hair back, ducks
down cellar and returns
wiping dust off a bottle:
old wine
to toast the New Year.

The Pipe

after Baudelaire

I am the pipe of an author;
you can tell by my colour,
Abyssinian or Kaffir,
my master is quite a smoker.

When he is feeling down,
I smoke like the cot
where a bubbling pot
awaits the ploughman's return.

I wrap his soul
in the tremulous blue net
from my fiery bowl,

I exude a powerful balm
to warm his heart,
and all his anxieties calm.

In Raymond's Barn

Useless cart slumped over its wheels,
a cat's cradle of cobwebs in what
was the manger, the paint-splotched

bench and a dozen pick-up-stick cages,
each containing a panicked thrush.
We have disturbed them, coming in.

Raymond knows each thrush by its song:
come hunting season
he'll truck them to a clearing, and wait

in a blind in the dwindling light
for the wild birds to land, lured
by the siren songs of his flock.

'But where's the pleasure' – Raymond's fist
funnels feed into each cage –
'where's the pleasure, if the hunter's grown deaf

to his decoys' songs?' He faces us,
shrugs, honest man's hands turned out –
'It's like a hound that can't bark.'

Two Varieties of Common Figs

In the beginning was the orchard
and your hands broad
as the fig tree's leaves

Noire de Caromb, *with 5 quite marked lobules, and the fruit
an elongated pear shape*
blackish fine and resistant skin of violet color, neck of reddish
    color slightly twisted, imperceptible stem,
flesh of amber pink color contrasted by the whitish rose of the
    thick filaments of the pistils

You peel me
slowly faster
you tip me up
all fours like a dog –
I almost bark
with pleasure.

*

And the second
a *Goutte d'Or*
we espaliered
on a morning after morning
suntrap of a wall
while in the background
the church bell
thumbed through
its book of hours

matins vespers or even
our heathen mid-morning snack:

magnificent golden figs to degust when ripe – a little drop
of juice hovers at the tip –

*

And thanks dear
for the hot sweet
coffee you brewed me
        after
to sip in bed
thighs parted
round the wet spots
on the sheet. Guess

I'll have to strip
the bed, this slab of
foam of no
polyurethane
on a platform
we assembled –
two-by-fours and
plywood, cheap
but

still bears well.

Degas' Bather

The orchards of the internet have rooms
for my virtual museums, and portals
to fancies I suppress: Roman revels
enhanced with sound effects, like my neighbour
this noon in his condo, earthquake water
stacked prudently on his porch,
a redwood between our double windows.

Sounds like he's surfed a porno flick. Her cries
ring out like waves and break
against our shingled walls. And here's the jug
she'll sluice her back with in a second
or a century: longing's embodiment
as I polish off my chicken breast, chased
with last night's wine, my foraged plum.

A Jar of Apricots after Chardin

Like the oval of a mirror the oils
show a sideboard chock-full of objects,
some almost transparent,
others stubbornly opaque.

The woman has stepped out for a moment
to fetch the missing ingredient,
or has she merely stepped back?
The mystery of her absence is compounded

by the pair of wine glasses: one barely touched
while behind it and darker
like a mirror image, the second is drained;

and the teacups, white porcelain. Steam rises
from the near one and a teaspoon's handle.
In the mirror – if there's a mirror – its double is pristine.

The Good Wife

Odysseus – the story goes – took a long trip, from Ithaca to
  Ithaca.

And she stayed home weaving the tapestry of her fidelity.

She was never tempted, they say, by apples, pomegranates, or
  other signs of a woman's frailty.

Now Odysseus is back. Once again Penelope demonstrates
  her resourcefulness.

Question: if she's so smart, why didn't she rid herself of the
  suitors?

It's the sort of question too literal children ask. *Why did
  Goldilocks? Why didn't Snow White?*

And the parents say – *It's only a story, it's late, go to bed, we
  have dishes to do.*

*

> Even once he dispensed with the suitors,
> showered and tossed his clothes in the wash,
> Penelope feared a god
> was hoodwinking her.
>
> Odysseus seethes. To the nurse he says:
> 'Find me some bedding. I'll sleep downstairs.'

'Prepare him the bed he built,'
Penelope corrects;

'take it to the hall. Heap it with fleeces
and the coverlets we weave on our looms . . .'
'What!' Odysseus shouts
– 'the bedstead I carved

from an olive tree, whose silvery leaves
quake like a virgin on her wedding night –
who would dare chop
my marriage bed from its root?'

*

So it *is* Odysseus, Penelope thinks.
After all these years.
She will miss her suitors. She looks
at Odysseus, looks at her wools
the tender green of the vine stock in spring,
blue-black like mildewy grapes
left on the vines when the pickers have passed:
fermented and sweet, almost wine.
What will she do now, without her suitors?

*

Penelope looks at Odysseus; looks at her unfinished tapestry.

Perhaps, she thinks, *a touch more carmine in the top right
corner.*

Near Knossos, A Borrowed House

From the next courtyard voices
argue. There's the old man, the
young man, the ingénue's treble –
grizzled patriarch; downy boy
whose lip is stained with a mustache;
a marriageable girl
some god has his eye on.

On and on, through the star-scarred night.
No parting shot, sealed with blood.
No slammed door, boots that clump
off. Not even the long, interrupted
silence of Amen, So-be-it.
I guess they've been at it for centuries,
like gods and the mortals.

Chestnut Trees in Croissy-sur-Seine

History has a view of the playing field,
chestnuts in waxy bloom, and the Seine,
which is out of bounds.

These kids are too big for her classroom.
They scuttle desks, fumbling for gear.
Something loud to bang, something sharp to stroke.

Out on the pitch playing football
they aren't awkard, they are dancers
who will never collide with a scrap

of shrapnel, who roll over and over on the green turf
coupled like lovers. The chemistry teacher
explains about gasses, how lungs dissolve

like candy floss on the tongue and you drown;
he reads a poem by Wilfred Owen
and exits with his models of gas molecules:

green for chlorine, yellow for sulfur,
mustard gas like a jungle gym. Pupils
hunch over their written work – July '16,

death tolls abstract as sums.
We must go, learn with our hands
like the blind: pat the good dog

artillery, fondle bayonets, pace
off the long divisions of graves
while our fingers tot up the plus signs.

Eve Goes Back

Some official document she needed,
tax quittance maybe
her certificate of birth –
she shuffles towards the checkpoint

shoes in hand. Why did they leave?
No time to pack – she recalls – and
how the angel cradled
an automatic weapon.

Interrogation, the routine
humiliation – stifled cries
like sex, like birth: expulsed from
(some concertina-wired town)

like the bodies she sees
on the world's front page
dumped like dirty clothes
in front of the machine.

Aphasia

Words make suffering more precise.
For hunger, any lover will tell you
gutturals are quite as effective.
In one stroke, your speech functions erased.

We spoon cake into your mouth.
Ah says Mouth. Good Boy!
we shout. Lexicons of emphasis,
dumb silences.

More sweet? we plead.
Eventually it goes down.
Mutely we gesture towards the shade.

Chin nods onto Chest. Body replenishes
Lungs, that sigh like reeds thinking
the thoughts they have no words for.

Côtes du Ventoux

We came, long after dark, but with the full moon lending us its friendly
light, to the little inn we'd left that morning before dawn.
– Petrarch, *Ascent of the Mont Ventoux.* Malaucène, 26 April 1336.

1

The village church rings the hour then
rings it again. The mistral rises.
From the mulberry, a leaf lets go –
hesitates – tries to climb back up.

Through barer branches now I see
my neighbour's lights. Does she see me
here under a bare-bulb moon,
tin guttering of the attic roof?

Good for the insomnia, this camping
out. A plane blinks south,
towards Marseilles. From where I lie

it bores right through the Dipper's side.
I roll over, tuck my knees
under my chin. Old tin pot. Old grief.

2

We tap on the pane, a voice quavers
from the scrubbed hearth. *It's us*, we call
through the door. *Can we come in?*
Carpet slippers scuff across cement tile.

She was reading
advertising leaflets dropped on the sill.
We lay another on the table, and
cakes from the bakery, Malaucène.

– *We came to say goodbye.*
– *Sit down a moment.* – *Madame Carle, we can't.*
We want to walk in the vineyards before dark.

A tear extrudes, like resin from bark.
Her finger stoppers it. We bend to kiss her.
– *Look after yourselves. Don't be gone too long.*

3

Out on the street, we look at each other,
about-face. – *Madame Carle, we're back.*
We can sit down a moment.
(I should call my mother tonight.)

– *I was crying,* she says – *Yes,* I say . . . *you know*
I polished our table so it would shine
like yours. She lifts a corner of the cloth:
Well you need to use beeswax and do it

every week. Skeptical, she lets the cloth drop.
Table, walnut sideboard with its sheaf
of everlastings and cluster of photographs

fill the room. – *About death, I don't care,
it's not seeing them.* She looks at Daniel
and Annie, Frédéric and the new child.

4

Did I snitch it from an album? Mum
leans against a log, arm
looped round my kid sister. They smile,
or laugh? At this distance, I no longer hear.

That's me perched on the log's big end,
sandaled heels drumming down. Sulking? Maybe.
Dad sits apart. Grandmother sits
on the plaid rug, surrounded by food.

Proud, I flashed the balloon, milky treasure
culled from the scum of tide.
Drop that! someone calls urgently. *Drop it –*

echoes. Behind us, the hillside smoulders,
but we don't know yet. So: memories
are burned – our unreliable narrators?

5

My grandfather whitewashed a barn
and strung good cord across it. No electricity
of course, we used coals. Grandmother
ironed for the whole village. When I married

she gave me two sheets – oh not embroidered
like some, we'd no time for fancy work.
The ironed sheets were hung on a line.
The water in the stream was always clean.

What a sight, their moon glow across our barn!
She never mixed anyone's up.
Only they were so rough they scorched my skin.

They are upstairs still, laid away.
Linen and cotton, folds as thick
as heavy cream. I'll never use them, those wedding sheets.

6

Joining the dots I flesh out Orion,
Madame Carle's winter-apple face,
Ursus, the soup-plate galaxies
like strings of suburbs, house lights left burning.

There, house-coat buttons she stitched back.
There, lace curtains, a pair of birds
freshly starched. *Touch them –*
the cry of a peacock is soft as wood ash.

Mother picks up the phone on the bedside table.
Betty or Bonnie will be there soon.
I'm ready, she says, *for the next thing,*

I need to pee. Glad you called, sweetie.
Click – she's off, receiver crooning
its cosmic tune. I lay it back in the cradle.

New Year

Panes of winter sunlight
jiggle on the wall – imperturbable
as hour hands, they advance
across the picture your mother
pinned there – a small
round garden table and slatted chair
back draped with a shawl,
shade collected in hollows
of ankle-deep grass. Still actual,
this C19 summer afternoon
ideal of happiness. Sun slants
round a corner, down the hall.

In Druid time I watch
the window of winter sunlight
gild our wall
and slurp my mug of coffee
thinking,
The days are growing longer now.

The Seine at Port Marly

When the noise in my head won't stop
and I hear that owl that hoots in the dark
– talking in her sleep perhaps –
I count up birds I observed on my walk,
beginning with the black-robed crow
presiding in the oak, impeccable magpie,
woodpecker belabouring a point –

not omitting the peaceable doves,
a glory of finches and my favourite,
the tiny European robin, whose
red breast glows like a cigarette tip.

Still wired? So tack on what you spotted
rowing this autumn – brooding cormorants,
blue heron scarfing down a fish,
model family of mallards – and that fox
afoot on the opposite bank, silhouette
dipped in silt where the river subsided,
nose pricked, ears pricked, tail oh! – tail

barely breathing in the blatant quiet
of an evening that deliberately dims
all but the eyes, and the ducks' dumb quaking
quacking for help.

The Owls

after Baudelaire

Snug in black yews they wait
sagely on a branch, like a row
of foreign gods now
darting a red eye. They meditate.

Motionless they will remain
until the melancholy hour
when pushing slant sun lower
the darkness swaggers in.

Their attitude instructs the wise
that in this world they'd best dissent
from turmoil and surprise;

those who each flitting shadow chase
are apt to bear the punishment
for having wanted to change place.

Polar Route

Breathless ends with a betrayal, Belmondo
sprinting from a cop
as Seberg runs her thumb across her lower lip
the way Belmondo used to.

If the sky falls now, Chicken Little,
it will fall on Saskatchewan.
Miles below our jumbo's porthole
one ploughed road, straight as a line

ruled across a sheet of foolscap –
white, far as the eye can see.
'Still Canada?' Berlin dude asks me.
I feel queasy, as if the map

of my life unfurled beneath the wing.
'Saskatchewan . . . where I was born.'
The wash froze on the line,
my Nan jotted that morning

in a diary I've stowed in a drawer
along with a wallet, gravid
with snapshots dad carried
through the four years of war.

Clear skies, our cheerful captain
announces, to our destination.
Time to watch another movie,
maybe *Annie Hall* or *Gravity*.

Sea to Sea

It was the railroad heyday, and they just
kept riding west,
first to the Prairies, then to the Coast
when they retired / tired of winter:
Glasgow Charlottetown Guelph and Saskatoon,
Crofters Salt Smugglers Sabbath Breakers
turned Loggers Wheat Farmers Shopkeepers.
Mother says *I miss the prairie skies*
I feel hemmed in by the mountains. The sea
at the door. We track sand in, we get swept out.
Great Uncle Sandy who emigrated
from Perth took us curling. We liked
the stone worn smooth by wind, like how his broom
kept the ice free of obstacles.
Nasturtiums tumbled over front walks,
leaves round as spare change I filched
from mother's purse, one beaver nickel
at a time, that way the level stayed the same.
In the drawer with her change purse and keys,
penny wise pound foolish she'd frown,
was a ball of string I unwound
just to see – more and more string, bound tighter.
Naturally, it was Mother I was after.

Granddad was a gardener, peas, spuds
and shrub roses bedded out of the shade
of the Garry Oaks: Moose Jaw Vancouver
where the train white with snow flees winter . . .
The nasturtiums were yellow and orange

and free. I pocketed seeds, sucked
nectar from the spur in the flower's back.
Grandmother grew up milking cows
on Prince Edward Island, headed west
with two of her sisters. She kept a bouquet
on the pedestal table along with
the miniature set of Shakespeare, porcelain
furniture reduced to the size of a fingerprint.
She was a teetotaler, I learned from mother,
who keeps her Scotch under the kitchen sink.

Strange, I think now – but sensed
even then? – how we replicate
in mirrors, gewgaws, books on a table
eye level with the voluptuous flowers
and tables in rooms that I walk through still;
how we strip away the layers, but
never find the bottom of anything.
I scrape at permafrost, unearth something,
whisk it off . . .
nasturtium nose tweaker nose twister,
let's put the *bird bath* here too,
granite churches named after John Knox.

If I assemble, pell-mell, these things, *words*,
that I think of, perhaps mistakenly,
as memories, memories
being what I mean when I say *my life*,
is it because I want to keep them –
like the nasturtiums, yellow and free,
that never seemed to stop flowering?
Do I think I can discover the child

who squats the strip of grass between house and world,
weighing her handful of seeds?
'What are you doing?' I ask her –
she looks at me like a stranger.

Medical History

The day you left the hospital without your undies. Much nicer –
you now know – without them, especially sub-zero days.
Wind chill factor.
What was it they cut out? You ought to tell them about that.
         Old X-rays, take them.
Maternal grandmother – what age did she . . . ?
Metastasis. Remember the last Chihuahua
         embalmed on the sofa?
Date of birth: forty below. *The laundry froze on the line*
         but she didn't miss a bridge game.
Tonsillectomy! Etherised! Snow wisping off a bald spot!
Count to ten the doctor said, you got to six.
         No baldness on our side of the family.
Don't forget the drugs: Paxil, Ambien, Hydrocodone, Valium.
All / none of the above.
Allergies? Penicillin? Alcohol? Smoke? Addictions?
Your mother, the something they removed. The lining of the something.
You could ask if she's forgotten.
         Dementia, definitely.
She left his long johns all night on the line. A touch of frost before dawn.
Your dad would know.
Side effects. All that itching. Awful way to go. Hear those sea lions
         rutting on the beach?
Heart ache   heart ache   heart ache   heart ache   heart ache   heart
   ache   heart.

I'll make a list, beginning with the bunions.

I Haven't Forgotten

after Baudelaire

I haven't forgotten our little house,
white and tranquil, though the city was close,
its plaster Pomona and old Venus
hiding their naked limbs in the bushes,
and the sun at evening cascading down,
knocking its ripe sheaf against our pane.
A great eye open in the curious sky,
it seemed on our quiet dinners to spy
and like candlelight spread its reflections
over the frugal cloth and serge curtains.

A Bunch of Daffs

I dropped the vase,
the daffs
we picked together
in Produce at Thrifty –

waists cinched by an elastic band,
yellow eyes askance.
They'd open,
I promised, in the north

light from the window
overlooking Georgia Strait's
crinkled tinfoil
waves, float planes

bumbling past
like the one I'm strapped in,
nose pressed
to the pane, looking out at you

wedged in the door
to the waiting room,
small, white-haired, impatient –
waving me off.

But also record the day
– halfway to the car –
you turned back to grumble,
'Love ya', as the kids say.'

Tennyson in December

J. P. – the signature on the flyleaf
and underneath, affiliations layered
like a dig through an encampment of the past,
University of S –;
   and under that – *CAS.*

   Heavens! What's *CAS?*

Well, still time to ask . . . maybe today
when I call to jog your memory
about the package you haven't claimed.
I've lost the notice, you object;
Think where you've been, I prompt,
but you can't you won't you say It
Doesn't Matter. *Don't treat me like a child*:
your voice shrugs off my arm.
When I want help I'll ask for it.

The frontispiece has an engraving
under tissue paper of a faun-eared
Tennyson, and the title page says

THE WORKS OF
ALFRED LORD TENNYSON
POET LAUREATE
MACMILLAN AND CO. LIMITED
ST. MARTIN'S STREET, LONDON
1932

Another thing I *took*, afraid
it would be culled in the next transhumance –
Assisted Living Skilled Nursing
Somewhere Else. I run my finger
over your marginalia –
'Alexandrine!' 'Free verse!' 'Xmas bells!!!'
'To strive, to seek, to find, and not to yield'
underlined twice. Odysseus our Mother?

How much I thought I knew I now know less.
A book, a button box, the keys –
to what? Remains painstakingly
exhumed from Arctic permafrost.
'In this hut the Dorset women
must have gathered to stitch skins,'
the museum reconstruction instructs
visitors who expect context
with the artifacts. Here's my diorama –
Print-Age Woman scans the obits
till the digits on the oven clock
assemble for a shot of Scotch.
I'm not an alcoholic yet.
If I stitch these remnants together
will I understand the reasons at last?

I'll call. About the chocolates.
Of the box I shipped in March
two still brood over their crib
of Easter grass: *They're big – I can
only eat a half at a time.*
                    And CAS – ?
In your old Tennyson? Green, leather bound?

$2.50 in the upper right
in someone else's rounder hand (did she
buy it secondhand . . .)? But I stop – afraid
you'll say, *It's mine, I want it back.*

Rests and Remains

My goodness you do go through a lot of

That's not where those dishes

If I've told you once I've

Your father and I could never have allowed ourselves to

I don't put knives in the

I wish you wouldn't fill the kettle that full it

After all if I'm paying for the phone call you might at least

Let's not have an

What were you doing down there on the beach were you

Level Crossing

watching a train of thought whoosh past
are you the only idling driver
who toys with the taffeta blue folds of summer sky,
envisaging a splotch of road-kill on the tracks;
are you the only one
whose thought stalls
out ahead of the steel apron in the fractious second
before it sweeps up all the pretty matchbook houses
porches picket fences automated
sprinkling systems chicken thawing where you left it
on the kitchen counter
with the packs of snacks, in case the boys are hungry
when they troop back from milking the Holstein herd,
trialing a cancer drug,
and you – you're stuck
at the crossing, third car back, waiting for the bells to stop?
        There, it's passed.
It's safe to cross now
but – LOOK BOTH WAYS! – you never know,
one thought may hide another.

Herring Run

She winces at the hand
navigating her up crazy pavement
through driving rain
to the captain's chair at the burl table
before the fireplace festooned
with gill nets. The herring spawn is on,
Qualicum Bay floodlit, boats
vying for spots, gulls
wheeling round like scraps
of paper buffeted by wind.

I'll never eat this, she says
to the plate of fish and chips, the coleslaw scoop:
*I asked for a child's portion
and ketchup not tartar sauce.
I need to go to the bathroom*, sotto voce.

Standing in the sentry box
of space outside the unlatched door,
over the quiet hecatomb
of herring trapped in mega nets,
I ask, *Do you need help?*

and whatever you feel you disguise
as irritation at my hovering,
flinching at the hand on your elbow
steering you back
to the child's portion before the fireplace
the ketchup bottle turned on its head.

Movie Night at Sunrise Manor

'Island at War, Part II' tonight,
though, if she saw Part I, mum's forgotten.
It feels like yesterday, their War.
On walkers and canes they press
from pudding to the Social Room,
Please Don't Disturb the Jigsaw Puzzle,
and some of them are English, girls
who wed Canadian soldiers and
washed up in this island beach town's
Sunrise Manor, Offering a Slate
of Lifestyle Options, So Nice To Come Home To.
Mrs P. is late again. A flirt the other
ladies snub, she stumbles in the dark
looking for a seat
as the enemy invades a Channel Isle,
French prostitutes are boated in.
The bike of the wife of the local bailiff
has a flat; a German officer stops,
offers to help repair it. In another world
they might be friends,
he's a decent man, she's hiding someone.

Cut to the party scene. Most local girls
will go, it's awfully dull with all
their brothers gone and the occupiers
are quite handsome in their uniforms
and only following orders.
Decking the village hall they sing
the songs her mother used to sing

along with the radio, ironing
and folding and putting away clothes.
Now mum is baffled by the plot –
why are things so muddled up?
Resistance? She wrote the script.
Get me out of here, she barks,
At Sunrise It's All About Choices.
She struggles to stand as the other roses
fading from the chintz sofa
fire off a disapproving *shush*.

Reader, forgive their commotion.
What good is Patience in the end,
A Bus For Outings And Appointments,
A Pond With Carp and Water Lilies?
They cannot pause, rewind, replay.
Television is a novelty
they rented for the Coronation.

Thought Is a Body of Water

Just now it comes back to me – this story I was translating, about a person trapped in a Garden, bombs falling, the father delayed.

*

Suddenly I am back where I sat translating the tale (tale of a Garden and something beyond; sometimes a bomb lands in the Garden):

*

I am back in the pub on the estuary; seaplanes landing and taking off. A hockey match on TV. My small white Mac with its out-of-date operating system. Amber beer, a white head.

(I want to cram as much as I can into this pub.)

The story is set in Algeria. The narrator holds a fistful of sand.

*

I am in my mother's house. On the other side of the same body of water. Small planes buzz past. The bald eagle's house of sticks. Computer on the sofa. Mother in hospital.

'As *stream* and *brook* are the boundaries of *river* in thinking, so the phenomenological world is only meaningful because we can think of something else that bounds it.'

We need the concept of nothingness in order to understand the concept of being, the philosopher says.

*

The fireplace, the hockey sticks, the hard, black puck. The Fraser River Delta's rich alluvial mud. *Mud*, root *muddle* . . . root *mother*?

A room on the other side of the same body of water.

I'm a little muddled, she says. Or, *I had such fun with you guys.*

Here is the known . . . experienced with the senses. Here is the unknown of which I can only conceive:

her absence.

The Origin of Art

Near Corinth, Pliny has it, lived a girl
whose love promised to be true
as he sailed off on business for a while,

winds uncertain. She lit a lamp
and cast his shadow on the wall,
next she drew a line around him.

Her dad, a potter, made a model
of the profile he fired with his pots –
Now you can hold love's silhouette.

So sculpture started, Pliny says,
to let us hold the pictures
we project upon our walls. Pliny says

a line marks the end of something,
a horizon, border or extremity
that keeps the figure from the background,
    our losses in the offing.

Black Box

Each evening when I'm done
(Bonnie sorts blister-packs
of pastel pills into a pop-up
tray, it's like a jewel box –

or no, more like the one dad kept
his flies for steelhead fishing
in), *when I say*, 'Goodnight Joan,'
she says, 'Thanks for nothing.'

We're on The Third Floor now:
pat-a-cake not bridge games
kill time. Church visitors bring
shade plants whose names

like me she almost remembers.
Wish I hadn't heard her shout
Shut your face! at the nurse. Oh, Bonnie, lock the box
before the bad words all fly out

and leave us only Pain.

La Sagrada Familia

We tell our stories to finish them
off, assign guilt, try to forgive
ourselves. *Let it go*, the listener

admonishes, with a glance at her watch,
with those matches
small fingers get burnt.

Metaphors, metaphors.
Gaudi's Nativity: this is a *family*,
no blessings withheld;

and the *sky*! – the ceiling I mean –
first light shines a prism in Eden
and all the beasts come to be named.

Gaudi: what a stickler, day
and night in the crypt of his shop – *finish?*
why finish? Isn't *time*

the construction? *My client*,
he says, leafing an arch,
my client is not in a rush.

The Sleep of the Magi

Gislebertus hoc fecit

They bivouack in Autun Cathedral.
The sculptor draws a sheet
around them, wrinkled as a pond

when a stone skips and
the shock rings expand,
fraying a little. Three heads on one pillow,

they've kept their crowns –
how could we know them,
without their crowns?

*

One stares into the dark.
Doesn't see the Angel
standing behind, index finger
wagging at the star

that looks like a flower.
It went behind a cloud
and they lay down
to wait for it to clear up, so tired

of journeying that Gabriel,
whose wings are like the fish-scale tile
of a Burgundy mansion,
has come to wake them.

Travelling Light

'*There are many things Place Saint-Sulpice*' – Georges Perec

From the town hall the quarter hour
plinks its coin of sound
into the already richly polluted air

and the sacristan opens the church,
looks up the rue Servandoni
to the *Bon Saint Pourçain*,

plats-du-yesterday still chalked
on the slate. Sun sweeps
the niches of the saints and martyrs, dusts

off pigeons. The sacristan
eyes the big box shelter
erected overnight on His Porch, raps – oh

gently – on the origami roof.
And soon enough the sleeper
rises, folds his nesting boxes

flat as a freshly ironed shirt
he tucks behind a drainpipe
for safekeeping till tonight.

Stations in the Metro

She dozes in the Metro. *Sèvres-Babylone*
under the Bon Marché, and Hôtel Lutetia,
requisitioned by Nazis, 1940. Nose in a book? –
alarms buzz – the train doors
are closing. She is lost in – what? –

                         was she reading
or was she looking at reflections
of reflections of other passengers
entering and exiting? Up above – ?
Oysters in straw. Badinage. Wine, maybe iced
champagne. *Lèche-vitrine lèche-cul* . . . it's not her station
yet.

I want this to happen in a second
on the page. But the mind keeps thinking other things.
Ironing half done in the kitchen.
Toaster on the blink. The alarm
a persistent stinging. Two girls, macaws
in a monkey puzzle jabbering, fall silent, gape – this is –
this was –
their station! *Ayee!* They leap –
opposite directions. The doors
are closing, will they, will they
not, get off? The buzzing –
stops. *Whew!* they're out
safe on the platform, ten steps between them,
arms raised – gawps of disbelief, then shrieks
of laughter, and now – nanoseconds –
they fall into each other's arms. *Exeunt.*

With a heave the train starts rolling.
A man refolds his *Figaro*; across
the aisle, this guy,
hair gelled into stiff peaks. Looks like
the icing mum made for that cake she baked,
soufflé-light, made from scratch
                              (mixes anathema)
eggs cracked, yolks set aside, whites whipped
'until they form stiff peaks', sugar
folded in . . . *Angel Food*. 'More,' we
plead, holding out our plates. 'More cake.'

Gell Guy plucks an earbud, a blue- or black-
berry, from the bush of his ear, and song
starts to leak into the train, picking up speed now,
leaping through tunnels like
trains of thought leaping through our brains.
Our eyes meet, we laugh out loud together –
those two girls – we think – we both are thinking –
what fantastic comic timing! Happy Days! Then
we're in the next lit station, *Rue de Rennes*.

Passers-by

after Baudelaire

Deafening, the traffic roared all around.
Slender, wearing black, regal in her grief,
a woman flits past, her elegant hand
lifting, swishing her skirt's flounce and its pleats;

light-footed, long-legged as a model.
I sat guzzling, grotesque as a gargoyle;
in her eye, livid sky where thunder builds,
intoxicating sweetness, pleasure that kills.

One flash – then the night! – Sudden beauty
who jolts me to life: won't I see
you again, except in eternity?

Too far! Too late! *Never* maybe.
Where do you fly to? And where do I go?
O you I could love – as, Lady, you know!

Smartphone

Look at her go, pedalling away from us
who lag behind and shout
'Don't stop, don't stop, don't stop!'

over stones and dirt blurred with new grass
and stiff grey sagebrush
we crush between our fingertips and sniff.

Send.

Two Friends One Gingko Three Marigolds

for Nancy Wilson and Nelee Langmuir

Lifting the latch I trespass: isn't that
your rake heaping up the gingko fans? No –
Doppler effect of cyclists swooping past,
gaudy as macaws. Back home, taped
to my ill neighbour's door –up three steps past three pots
of marigolds – three terracotta gods –
the white sheet of foolscap has a red
felt-tipped heart and in blue 'Welcome! Come in!'

But you can't be far. Running errands?
Unstinting your roses bloom – *Earth Song*, *Breath of Life*,
Tipsy Imperial Concubine. Beside
the compost, the watering can. I tweak
the wind chime. Close the gate
against those other trespassers, the long-eared mule deer.

The Girl Next Door Knocks at the Door

A garden rose is her desire, being
herself an ancient species, flesh and treacherous
but pink and practical, eyes
forget-me-not. We snip a rose

that's opening, petals lipstick-smudged.
Strip thorns – no vicious prick
shall send this princess off to sleep a century.
Your bud needs water, I say – go

stick it in a glass. She loves me she loves me
not she strips each velvet petal off
discards it like a losing card. She loves me

not. Click clack the shutter of her smile – oh neat
white teeth! Roses in her cheeks!
Skin deep is deep enough for me.

'A Day in the Life of a Chair'

after a print by Judith Pressey

I have a life, too-eee.
Nylon-webbed aluminum tubing, light –
lift me, you can, crook a finger!

But I'm strong, yes ma'am. I'll hold
you after hours on the porch,
kink in your neck from standing staring

at that clump of earth, mama's breast.
Running your hands
through the sky's milky skeins. A dome

of mountain in a scrim of mist, orange
as an orange popsicle.
Moonlight turns the porch to eye shadow.

Empty I drop off the world. Uh huh, like that.
Pack up flat as a set of Minoan
bones packed in a cedar-wood chest.

Grace Notes

Birch trees
perform their long striptease
chickadees

airbrush the catkins
to the carport's tarpaper roof overnight rain
imparts a sheen

gold leaf tangles
of electric cables
voicemail
from a passing gull

a strand of tinsel
shimmies in the breeze the usual
frisky squirrels
catwalk their tails

Unfinished

I've set today aside
to write the poem
about love, the one
in which I'll define

the questions. But first
I make some tea,
a brand new packet
with Chinese characters –

a poem? a landscape
whose small figures won't ever reach the peak
if there's a peak
behind that cloud?

Under scrub pines
they brew tea. Flowers unfurl
steam
fragrant as bees.

> The phone that black lobster
> rings – my daughter
> stuck in a blizzard, airport
> clogged with travellers, all

> the outlying
> floodlit football fields effaced.
> No flights
> out tonight.

I sip black tea
turned cold. Boot up
my computer but
how to launch my poem

when love
my daughter's a thousand miles away
unequipped for snow?
I rummage through a drawer

for mittens, the pair
with strings attached.
Tomorrow I swear
I'll unplug it – my old landline, cord

coiling across the floor
of oceans – before I try
to write the poem –
the definitive – on love.

(B) *editions*

Founded in 2007, CB editions publishes chiefly
short fiction (including work by Will Eaves,
Gabriel Josipovici, David Markson and
May-Lan Tan) and poetry (Beverley Bie Brahic,
Nancy Gaffield, J. O. Morgan, D. Nurkse, Dan
O'Brien). Writers published in translation include
Apollinaire, Andrzej Bursa, Joaquín Giannuzzi,
Gert Hofmann, Agota Kristof and Francis Ponge.

Books can be ordered from www.cbeditions.com.